Understanding
Cycles and
Systems

Andrew Solway

Chicago, Illinois

www.heinemannraintree.com
Visit our website to find out more information about Heinemann-Raintree books.

To order:

☎ Phone 888-454-2279
🖳 Visit www.heinemannraintree.com to browse our catalog and order online.

Edited by Sabrina Crewe
Designed by Sabine Beaupré
Original illustrations © Discovery Books 2009
Illustrated by Stefan Chabluk
Picture research by Sabrina Crewe
Originated by Discovery Books
Printed and bound in China by CTPS

14 13 12 11 10
10 9 8 7 6 5 4 3

Library of Congress Cataloging-in-Publication Data
Solway, Andrew.
  Understanding cycles and systems / Andrew Solway.
    p. cm. -- (Sci-hi. Earth and space science)
  Includes bibliographical references and index.
  ISBN 978-1-4109-3348-5 (hc) -- ISBN 978-1-4109-3358-4 (pb) 1. Earth sciences--Juvenile literature. 2. Earth--Juvenile literature. I. Title.
  QE29.S69 2008
  550--dc22
                      2009003531

Acknowledgments
The author and publishers are grateful to the following for permission to reproduce copyright material:
© European Space Agency/NASA p. **18**; © Getty Images pp. **12** (Michael Melford), **43**; © MODIS Oceans Group, NASA Goddard Space Flight Center p. **40**; © NASA pp. **28**, **41** left, **42**; © NASA/Goddard Space Flight Center p. **4**; © NASA/Boeing Company p. **41** right; © NOAA p. **22**; © SeaWiFS Project, NASA/Goddard Space Flight Center, and ORBIMAG p. **38**; © Shutterstock cover inset (Yellowj), pp. **3** top (Ron from York), **3** bottom (RCP Photo), **6** (Mark Lorch), **7** (Danny Warren), **8** (Jason Maehl), **9** (Armin Rose), **11** (Serg Zastavkin), **13** all, **14** both, **19** (Stepan Jezek), **21** (Ron from York), **24** (Planner), **26** (Russell Shively), **29** (Lorraine Kourafas), **30** (James Doss), **31** (Vera Bogaerts), **33** all, **34** (RCP Photo), **37** (Inc), **39** (George Muresan).

Cover photograph of the Icelandic Low, an area of low atmospheric pressure, is reproduced with permission of NASA.

We would like to thank content consultant Suzy Gazlay and text consultant Nancy Harris for their invaluable help in the preparation of this book.

Every effort has been made to contact copyright holders of any material reproduced in this book. Any omissions will be rectified in subsequent printings if notice is given to the publisher.

All the Internet addresses (URLs) given in this book were valid at the time of going to press. However, due to the dynamic nature of the Internet, some addresses may have changed, or sites may have changed or ceased to exist since publication. While the author and Publishers regret any inconvenience this may cause readers, no responsibility for any such changes can be accepted by either the author or the Publishers.

Contents

A Dynamic Planet   4

BGC Cycles   10

The Water Cycle   14

The Carbon Cycle   16

The Oxygen Cycle   22

The Nitrogen Cycle   24

The Rock Cycle   26

The Energy Balance   28

The Food Web   32

Air and Water   34

Learning from Satellites   40

Cycles, Systems, and Us   42

Cycles and Systems Quiz   44

Glossary   45

Find Out More   47

Index   48

What is the link beween the carbon cycle and floods? Find out on page 21!

Which one of Earth's systems causes waves? Find out on page 34!

Some words are shown in bold, **like this**. These words are explained in the glossary. You will find important information and definitions underlined, **<u>like this</u>**.

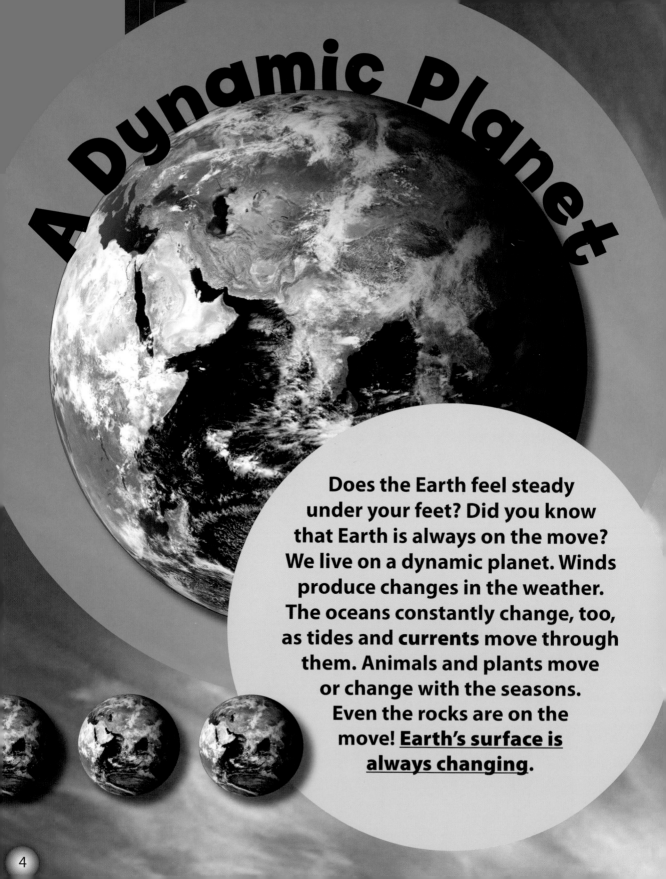

A Dynamic Planet

Does the Earth feel steady under your feet? Did you know that Earth is always on the move? We live on a dynamic planet. Winds produce changes in the weather. The oceans constantly change, too, as tides and **currents** move through them. Animals and plants move or change with the seasons. Even the rocks are on the move! <u>Earth's surface is always changing</u>.

Systems

These changes are Earth's natural processes, and they are parts of a **system**. A system is a group of connecting parts that works together. Some processes belong to several systems. A good way to learn about Earth is to look at its systems.

The most important system is the energy that powers all the other systems. This energy comes from the Sun. Another important system is the **atmosphere**, or the protective layer of gases that forms the air.

There are other "spheres," or systems, on Earth. The **hydrosphere** is all the water. The **biosphere** contains all living things. The term **geosphere** refers to the rocks and soils that form Earth's crust, or outer layer.

Cycles

Within Earth's systems, we can see repeating patterns that we call **cycles**. Cycles take place again and again. For example, water is constantly moving in a cycle between the oceans, land, and air. We call this the water cycle, and we are going to learn more about it and about other important cycles in our world.

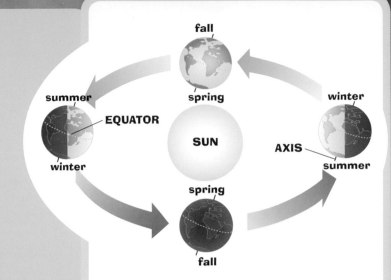

Seasons

Earth's seasons are a good example of a cycle. Earth orbits around the Sun once in every year. <u>The seasons change as Earth revolves around the Sun</u>. Different places get different seasons because Earth is tilted on its axis toward or away from the Sun. When a part of Earth is tilted toward the Sun, it gets more sunlight and is warmer. That period is the region's summer. Many areas have four seasons: spring, summer, fall, and winter. Other places close to the **equator** have only two: a wet season and a dry season.

Changing and changing again

Nearly all substances on Earth have been here since the planet was formed. But these materials do not stay still. They are always moving and changing form.

Before we look at the different cycles, let's learn a little about the processes that make Earth so dynamic. These processes cause the changes that take place in cycles and systems. They are changing everything all the time—even you!

All substances are made up of atoms and molecules. The **atom** is the basic **particle** (small piece). A **molecule** is a group of joined atoms. The atoms in a molecule can be the same, as in oxygen, which only has oxygen atoms. Or they can be different, as in water, which is made of oxygen and hydrogen atoms.

A guide to substances and symbols

An **element** is a simple substance made of just one kind of atom. **Carbon**, hydrogen, and oxygen are all elements. There are 92 known elements that occur naturally on Earth.

Each element has one letter or two letters as its chemical symbol. Oxygen is O, carbon is C, hydrogen is H, and helium is He. In oxygen's usual form, its atoms join up in pairs, and so its symbol is O_2. The little number 2 shows the number of atoms.

A **compound** is a substance made up of more than one kind of atom. Carbon dioxide is a simple compound. It has one carbon atom joined to two oxygen atoms, written as CO_2. (Sometimes it is written as O=C=O.) Two hydrogen atoms joined with one oxygen atom make water, so water's symbol is H_2O.

Chemical processes

In chemical processes, atoms and molecules react with each other and change. These processes are called **chemical reactions**. Certain chemical reactions are especially important to Earth's cycles. One is **photosynthesis**, a process in which plants use energy from sunlight to make their own food. We are going to learn more about photosynthesis on pages 16 and 22. You'll see how it fits in with several cycles.

People and animals use a chemical process to get energy and grow. Find out how on pages 22-23.

Combustion, or burning, is a chemical reaction. The carbon released by the burning wood reacts with oxygen in the air, and they join to become carbon dioxide.

How much water?

Water changes its form, but there is always the same amount of it. Altogether, there are about 1,400 million cubic kilometers (332.5 cubic miles) of water in the world. Nearly 97 percent of that water is saltwater. Only a tiny fraction is freshwater that people can use.

Physical processes

A physical process is one where substances stay basically the same. There is no chemical reaction. For example, water can **evaporate** (turn from a liquid to a gas) to form water vapor. It can also freeze to form ice. In both cases, however, it is still water. It has the same molecules as liquid water and can easily change back into a liquid.

Moving around

The different ways things move from one to place to another are important to the world's cycles. Every day, you can see things move around on Earth.

A fast-flowing river can carry along rocks and sand. The materials are deposited in another place, where they may settle or move again.

These hot springs in Yellowstone National Park, Wyoming, show how materials can move from one part of a cycle to another. The white rocks were formed from materials deep in the ground. Minerals from underground rocks dissolved in the hot spring water and were carried up to the surface.

Storing substances

Not everything is on the move all the time. Stores, or reservoirs, are places where materials build up, or **accumulate**. They may remain in a store for a long time. The Antarctic ice cap is a huge water store. It contains more freshwater than all the rivers and lakes in the world.

Other substances dissolve in the water and are carried along. This is how rivers carry **minerals** into the ocean. Minerals are natural, nonliving substances found in Earth's rocky surface. The most common minerals carried by rivers are sodium and chlorine, which combine to make salt. Over millions of years, rivers have gradually added more and more salts to the ocean. This is why seawater is salty!

Blown by the wind

The wind carries dust, sand, grit, and other particles from place to place. Winds also carry living things, such as pollen and seeds from plants. Gases also mix with the air and move with it when the wind is blowing.

BGC Cycles

As we just saw, materials can move physically from place to place. They can change physically, too. They can also change chemically, which means that their parts react and change. Substances can become part of living things. Then they can become part of rocks or water.

Many of these changes happen in **cycles**—they follow the same pattern and recycle the same materials. These cycles are known as **biogeochemical** cycles, or **BGC** cycles.

What is BGC?

• BGC stands for *biogeochemical*. *Bio* means living. Biological processes are things that happen in the living world.

• *Geo* means earth or rocks. Geological processes go on in the nonliving world.

• **Chemical processes are reactions between atoms and molecules** (the small parts that make up all materials). Every cycle on Earth is either biological, geological, chemical, or a mix of the three.

Earth's cycles and **systems** move materials from the air to water. These materials can also be part of living things and nonliving things.

Some BGC cycles

- **WATER** goes in a cycle from the sea to the **atmosphere** and back again. This is just one of the many ways in which water is recycled.

- **SEASONS** follow each other in a cycle as Earth goes around the Sun.

- **LIFE CYCLES** of plants and animals follow patterns of birth, reproduction, and death.

- **ROCKS** break down and re-form in cycles that can last millions of years.

- **CHEMICAL elements** such as oxygen, **carbon**, and **nitrogen** are essential to life. These elements move between the living and the nonliving worlds.

Driven by energy

All the different types of cycles are driven by energy. Without energy from somewhere, none of the processes would happen. **Living things get their energy from sunlight**. Plants make food directly from sunlight. Animals get their energy indirectly from sunlight. They do this by eating plants or other animals. This energy drives the animal's life cycle. On the next page is an example of the life cycle of an animal.

Reusing materials

BGC cycles are always recycling the substances in rocks, water, and living things. Materials may be used up in one process, but then they become a useful part of the next process in the cycle. When an animal dies, for example, some of its remains may become food for other animals.

BGC cycles are not simple circles, however. Each cycle is more like a network of different processes. We can see how this works by looking at several important cycles in the next few chapters.

Recycled breath

Take a couple of breaths. Now think of all the people who lived and breathed on Earth a few thousand years ago—the ancient Egyptians, for example. Tutankhamen was an ancient Egyptian king. Every time you breathe, there is a chance that you will breathe in part of Tutankhamen's last breath. The **molecules** in air are so tiny that his last breath contained about 10,000 billion billion of them! Since Tutankhamen's time, these molecules have been recycled many times.

The life cycle of a frog

2. After they hatch, tadpoles breathe and find food in the water.

1. Tadpoles form inside a clump of eggs in the water.

Different animal species follow different types of life cycle as they move from birth to death. But they all grow into adults and then reproduce. These pictures show different stages in the life cycle of a frog.

3. Tadpoles start to grow legs as they begin to turn into frogs.

5. Adult female frogs release eggs into the water. The male frogs fertilize the eggs.

4. Young frogs can breathe on land. They get their energy from eating insects and other small animals.

The Water Cycle

Earth is a watery planet. About 97 percent of that water is in the oceans. But there is also water in rivers and lakes as well as water underground (**groundwater**). There is water vapor (gas) in the air and frozen water (ice) at the Poles. Even living things are made mostly of water!

None of this water stays in one place for long. Several processes move water through the **hydrosphere** and recycle it. Together, they make up the water **cycle**.

Homemade water cycle

Put a small amount of water in the bottom of a bowl that is deeper than a coffee cup. Put an empty coffee cup in the middle of the bowl. Cover the bowl with food wrap. You can use a rubber band or string to hold it on more tightly. Put a small stone in the middle of the food wrap to make a dip over the mug. Then put the bowl in a sunny place for a few days. What happens? You should find that "rain" gradually builds up in the coffee cup.

The water cycle

When water vapor cools, it begins to **condense**, or turn back into a liquid. Condensing water forms clouds in the sky.

Evaporation happens when the Sun heats water and turns it into water vapor (gas). The water vapor becomes part of the atmosphere.

Surface **runoff** is the rain, melted snow, or other water that runs into rivers, streams, or other bodies of water. Eventually it will run into the ocean.

Condensed water falls to the ground as rain, snow, hail, or sleet. This process is called **precipitation**.

Vehicles and engines release water vapor into the air during **combustion**, which takes place when they burn fuel.

Accumulation happens when water collects, or accumulates, in oceans, seas, and lakes.

Plants take in water from the soil through their roots and release it through their leaves. This process is called **transpiration**.

Animals take in water when they drink and eat. They lose water vapor in their breath as they breathe out. This is known as **respiration**.

Infiltration happens when water soaks into the rocks below ground. The water is often stored as groundwater.

THE CARBON CYCLE

Carbon is an essential element in all living things. The carbon **cycle** is therefore a very important **BGC** cycle.

Why is carbon so important? It is the building block of all living material. **All plants and animals are made of carbon combined with other elements**. Carbon is also found in oceans, the air, and even in some rocks!

The ocean, air, soil, and living things constantly exchange carbon. This is the process we call the carbon cycle.

Carbon everywhere

Carbon has many forms. These include graphite, which is what the "lead" in a pencil is made of. Diamonds are made of carbon, too! So is the soot from a candle and the ash left after something burns.

Carbon explosion

Movement of carbon between the deep ocean and the ocean surface takes hundreds of years. But volcanic eruptions can cause an explosion of carbon! Volcanoes erupt in the ocean as well as on land. Volcanoes produce large amounts of gases, including carbon dioxide, which escape into the atmosphere.

The carbon cycle

There are more than 3 trillion metric tons (3.3 trillion tons) of carbon dioxide (CO_2) in the air. This is only **0.04%** of the total air!

When **fossil fuels** are burned, most of the carbon they held goes into the atmosphere.

Plants on land and in the ocean use CO_2 plus sunlight to make food through **photosynthesis**. The carbon becomes part of the plant. At night, plants release CO_2 into the air.

Animals release carbon dioxide during **respiration**.

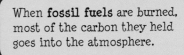

Animals get their carbon from the food they eat.

When plants die and decay, the carbon they contain is stored in their remains and gradually released into the ground.

Oceans absorb large amounts of CO_2 from the air.

Carbon is stored in rocks and in **sediments** on the ocean floor.

Remains of some plants and animals that died and were buried millions of years ago have turned into fossil fuels. The fossil fuels store carbon from the remains.

Carbon stores

The complex chemicals that make up living things are all based on carbon. Living things store, or keep, carbon in their tissues. For this reason, they are called **carbon stores**. The ocean, rocks, soil, and air are also carbon stores.

A carbon store can be either a sink or a source. A **carbon sink** is a store that takes up more carbon from the atmosphere than it releases. A **carbon source** is a store that releases carbon into the atmosphere.

Sediments in the ocean

The ocean bed is a huge carbon store. Many ocean animals make their shells from a mineral called calcium carbonate, which is rich in carbon. When the creatures die, the shells fall to the ocean floor. The remains of other marine animals also sink to the ocean floor and decompose. These remains become sediments (settled matter) on the ocean bed.

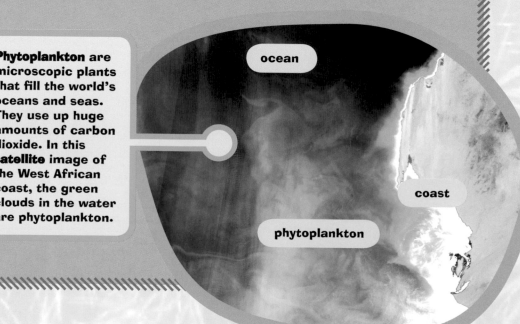

Phytoplankton are microscopic plants that fill the world's oceans and seas. They use up huge amounts of carbon dioxide. In this **satellite** image of the West African coast, the green clouds in the water are phytoplankton.

ocean

coast

phytoplankton

Trees are long-lived, so carbon can be locked up in them for hundreds or even thousands of years. But when trees are cut down and burned, their carbon is released.

Rock and fossil fuels

Limestone is another store of carbon. It is a rock that forms on the ocean floor from the remains of shelled ocean animals. Coal, oil, and gas are the remains of living things that existed millions of years ago. These fossil fuels are also large carbon stores.

The biggest carbon store

The oceans and seas are by far the biggest carbon store. They contain more than three-quarters of all Earth's carbon.

Carbon and climate change

Carbon dioxide (CO_2) is a greenhouse gas. Along with other greenhouse gases, it traps heat in the atmosphere. Without it, Earth would be frozen and nothing could live on it. But, like all natural cycles, the carbon cycle needs to be kept in balance. Too much CO_2 could cause the world to get uncomfortably warm.

NATURAL REMOVAL

Carbon is constantly removed from the atmosphere by the oceans and by forests and other vegetation. About half the carbon dioxide **emissions** (released substances) we produce are balanced by this removal.

Global warming

In the last 150 years, the amount of carbon dioxide in Earth's atmosphere has increased. Earth's surface temperature has also risen slightly over the same period. This rise in temperature, usually called global warming, has caused the **climate** to change.

Human activities

Scientists believe that this change is linked to the rise in carbon dioxide in the atmosphere. This rise is due to human activities. **People's actions affect the carbon cycle in more than one way**. Deforestation (cutting down forests) releases lots of carbon. So does farming. Deforestation and farming together release about 2 billion metric tons (2.2 billion tons) of carbon each year. Burning fossil fuels and industries (such as concrete making) add about 7 billion metric tons (7.7 billion tons) of carbon to the air each year. In 2008, about 10 billion metric tons (11 billion tons) of carbon were released into the atmosphere because of human activity.

Floods caused by heavy rainfall have hit British towns in recent years. Scientists say that global warming has caused the unusual weather.

Effects of climate change

Global warming causes the climate to change in several ways. We get warmer days and longer periods of hot weather. Lack of rainfall in some areas causes droughts, or water shortages. In other areas, heavy rainfall causes floods and loss of crops. Ocean **currents** change when water gets warmer. This change affects the climate. Ocean levels are rising as great bodies of ice on land melt into the ocean. Rising sea levels cause floods along coasts and rivers.

ThE OXYGEN CYCLE

Heavy oxygen

There is oxygen in rocks—a lot of it! Oxygen makes up almost half the weight of rocks. Most of this oxygen remains locked in the rocks for millions of years.

The oxygen **cycle** is the movement of oxygen among Earth's systems. Oxygen is the most common **element** on Earth. It moves in and among the **hydrosphere** (water), the **atmosphere** (air), the **biosphere** (living things), and the **geosphere** (rocks and soil).

Oxygen in the atmosphere

Do you remember reading about **chemical reactions** on page 7? Chemical reactions are the way that oxygen gets in and out of the atmosphere.

Most of the oxygen in our atmosphere comes from plants. Plants produce oxygen during the chemical reaction called **photosynthesis**.

Almost all animals get the energy for growing and surviving from the chemical process called **respiration**. During respiration, land animals take in oxygen, removing it from the atmosphere. Water animals use the oxygen dissolved in the water.

Deep ocean life

A few living things can survive without sunlight or oxygen. Deep in the world's oceans, openings in the ocean floor release hot, gushing water full of **minerals**. Some unique forms of life make their homes around these vents. They include tube worms (above), crabs, and very small fish. They live on **bacteria** that feed on minerals coming from the vents.

The oxygen cycle

During the process of photosynthesis, plants absorb carbon dioxide from the air and release oxygen into the atmosphere. Photosynthesis needs sunlight, and so it happens during the day. At night, plants take up oxygen from the atmosphere.

Some oxygen from the air dissolves in water. **Phytoplankton** (microscopic plants living in water) release oxygen during photosynthesis.

During respiration, land animals breathe in oxygen from the air and produce carbon dioxide and water.

When living things die, the process of decay uses up oxygen from the atmosphere.

Water animals take in oxygen from the water.

Most of the world's oxygen supplies are stored in rocks. Some oxygen is released when rocks are **weathered** (broken up by wind, ice, or rain).

The Nitrogen Cycle

All living things—including you—need **nitrogen** to grow. Plants absorb it from soil or water. Animals and people get this nitrogen from the plants or other animals they eat.

Nitrogen is an **element**. It is all around us in the **atmosphere** in the form of a gas. The nitrogen **cycle** is the movement of nitrogen from the atmosphere to animals, plants, and the soil.

In the air

About 80 percent of the air is made of nitrogen. But we don't use the nitrogen we breathe. We have to get our nitrogen from food.

Fixing nitrogen

Living things need nitrogen to survive and to grow. There is lots of nitrogen in the air, but most living things can't use this pure nitrogen. There are, however, a few kinds of **bacteria** that can use nitrogen in this form. They help other living things get nitrogen, too.

The microscopic bacteria that do this important job are everywhere in soil and water. The bacteria turn nitrogen into **compounds** that plants can use. This process is called nitrogen fixing. This is an important part of the nitrogen cycle because it's how plants and animals get the nitrogen they need.

Most nitrogen-fixing is done by bacteria, but some is done by lightning! The huge amount of energy in a flash of lightning can break up nitrogen **molecules** in the air. The process creates nitrogen compounds in the air.

The nitrogen cycle

Nitrogen compounds in the air fall to Earth in rain.

Lightning breaks up nitrogen in the air so it can combine with oxygen.

Wildfires cause extra nitrogen to be released into the air.

Farmers often use fertilizers that add nitrogen to the soil to make plants grow bigger and faster.

Plants get nitrogen from the soil or water in which they live.

Animals eat plants containing nitrogen. This nitrogen will return to the soil as waste material or when an animal dies and decays.

Nitrogen-fixing bacteria change nitrogen into compounds that other living things can use. Other bacteria convert nitrogen compounds in the soil into gas. Then they release nitrogen gas back into the air.

The Rock Cycle

Rocky nutrients

Living things need small amounts of **elements** to survive and grow. These elements include **minerals** such as phosphorous, sulfur, iron, and calcium. Living things such as lichens (simple plant forms) can break down rocks over many years. This process releases the minerals held in rocks. They become **nutrients** (substances that help things grow) in the soil.

Rocks are constantly but slowly changing form. What starts out as one type of rock may turn into another, taking millions of years to do so. What was a chunk of mountain may one day be a handful of sand. These changes are all part of the rock **cycle**.

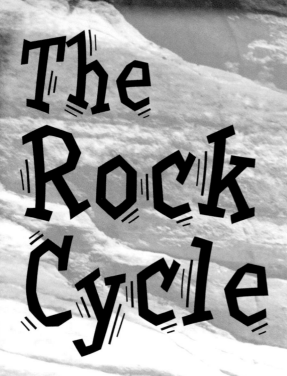

Rock layers form and shift over millions of years. Then **weathering** and **erosion** gradually alter rocks.

The rock cycle

Rock can be broken up or changed by wind, rain, snow, and ice. This process is called weathering.

Rock can be pushed up to the surface by slow movements of the Earth's crust (outer layer). Sometimes, magma is pushed up to the surface and erupts from a volcano.

Some weathered rock is carried away by wind, ice, or water. This is erosion.

The rock pieces made by weathering can vary in size from gravel (pea-sized lumps) to silt (fine powder). When these pieces settle, they become **sediment**.

Sediments are carried by rivers to the ocean. Layers of sediment collect on the ocean floor.

Over time, older sediments are buried by newer ones. They are compacted (squashed), and water is squeezed out. Over the course of millions of years, the sediments slowly turn into **sedimentary rock**.

If sedimentary rocks become buried deep enough, they get hot and compacted. Then they change into **metamorphic rocks**, such as slate or marble.

When magma cools down and hardens, it becomes **igneous rock**. If igneous rocks receive extreme heat and pressure, they become metamorphic rock.

Deep underground, some rocks get so hot that they melt completely and become **magma**.

The Energy Balance

Energy is what keeps Earth alive. Without it, this would be a dark, dead planet. The world is bathed in energy that comes from the Sun. This energy powers all of Earth's **cycles** and **systems**.

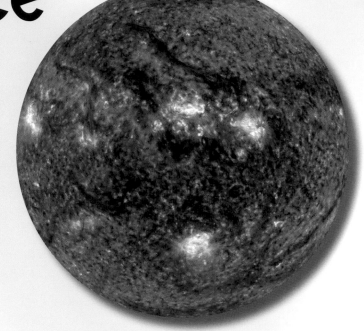

Energy from the Sun

The Sun pours out huge amounts of energy. The energy that reaches us is **radiation**—energy given off in invisible waves, or rays. Most of these rays are either light or **infrared** rays (heat).

The air absorbs some of the Sun's energy before that energy reaches the ground. This warms the atmosphere.

UNEVEN HEATING

Different parts of the world get different amounts of the Sun's energy. Areas close to the **equator** generally get more energy than areas close to the North and South poles. This is why the **climate** is warmer near the equator than near the poles. The uneven heating causes winds and ocean **currents** (see pages 36–41). In fact, **all weather is the result of uneven heating of Earth**!

What happens to the Sun's energy when it reaches Earth?

When sunlight does reach Earth's surface, a lot of it is absorbed by the land or the sea. The sunlight warms up the rocks or water. The rocks and water then radiate (give out) heat. This helps to warm the air close to the ground.

The sea absorbs a lot more heat than the land. Water is able to hold a lot of heat. Land areas heat up more quickly, but they cool down quicker, too.

About 30 percent of the Sun's energy is reflected straight back into space. It bounces off the atmosphere, the clouds, or Earth's surface. About 19 percent is absorbed by the atmosphere, clouds, or dust. About 51 percent is absorbed at Earth's surface by the land and the sea.

Sunlight for life

Living things also absorb the Sun's energy. Plants absorb a lot of sunlight. They use it to make their own food through **photosynthesis**. In the ocean, **phytoplankton** (microscopic water plants) do a similar kind of thing.

Absorbing sunlight also helps animals to keep warm. Cold-blooded animals, such as reptiles, especially rely on direct sunlight. When they get too cold, they can move only slowly. If they bask in sunlight, it warms up their bodies and they can move faster.

Melting ice

The Arctic region stays colder because it's covered with ice and snow. The white surface reflects the Sun's rays back into space. But when the ice melts, the land beneath is exposed. Dark areas absorb more heat. As Arctic lands warm from **climate change**, more ice is melting. More dark land is being exposed. The warming process speeds up and creates its own cycle.

Infrared images can show varying temperatures as different colors. The different colors in this infrared image show that the inner parts of the hand are warmer than the outer parts.

Red areas are the hottest.

Green and blue areas are the coolest.

Changing the balance

Usually, the energy received from the Sun is balanced by the heat escaping into space. So Earth should not get warmer or cooler. It should stay at about the same temperature.

In the past 150 years, however, humans have affected Earth's energy balance. When we burn **fossil fuels**, the **carbon** released into the air forms carbon dioxide. This carbon dioxide absorbs and holds heat. The increase of carbon dioxide in the atmosphere has upset the normal energy balance. Earth is absorbing more energy than it is losing. It is slowly getting warmer.

The Food Web

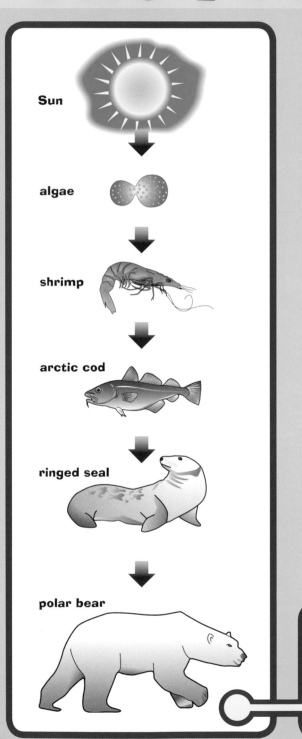

Sun

algae

shrimp

arctic cod

ringed seal

polar bear

Let's look at a system that puts cycles and energy together. Energy flows through living things in a system called the **food web**. A food web connects energy, plants, and animals. <u>**The energy from sunlight is changed into other forms of energy that living things need to survive.**</u>

Plants and **algae** use the Sun's energy to make food. When an animal eats a plant, some of the plant's energy passes to the animal. Animals pass on some energy when they are eaten by other animals.

As with other systems, the parts of the food web rely on other parts. On the next page, you can see how living things in the food web pass energy through the web as they become food for each other.

The food web is made up of many smaller **food chains**. In a food chain, the animal at the end gets its energy by eating the next animal in the chain. This food chain is typical in the Arctic region, where the Sun's energy passes from algae all the way to polar bears!

Plants absorb carbon dioxide from the air. As we learned on page 18, carbon is an important building block of living things. Plants use photosynthesis to change carbon dioxide into food for growth.

Herbivores are animals that eat plants. They turn some of the plant carbon into animal **tissue**. The rest is used in **respiration**. It goes back into the atmosphere as carbon dioxide.

Carnivores eat other animals instead of plants. Omnivores eat both plants and animals. These animals turn some of the carbon from their food into new animal tissue and release the rest through respiration.

Scavengers are creatures that feed on dead and rotting tissue. They get their food when an animal or plant dies. Scavengers include blowflies, cockroaches, and vultures. Scavengers break dead material down into small pieces of **biomass**. Biomass is any matter that comes from living things, such as dead animals and plants.

Decomposers get to work on biomass. The main decomposers are earthworms and various kinds of **bacteria** and fungi (plantlike life forms that live off other things). They break down the complex chemicals in the dead material into much simpler substances. These simple substances are released into the soil.

The movement of winds around Earth causes waves to form on the ocean.

Air and Water

The atmosphere and the oceans are never still. Waves are constantly moving across the ocean surface. Ocean currents carry water thousands of miles. Winds range from gentle breezes to howling hurricanes. Where does the energy come from to power all this movement?

Different amounts of energy

Our seasons, winds, weather, and ocean currents all exist because of the Sun's energy. As we saw on page 28, areas near the **equator** get more energy than areas near the poles. The amount of energy an area receives also varies with the seasons.

This uneven heating is the main driving force behind the movements of air and oceans. It creates **convection** currents. The spin of Earth also affects the way that the air and water **systems** move.

ALL ABOUT CONVECTION CURRENTS

Convection is one type of heat transfer (movement from one place to another). To work, convection needs a difference in temperature. It also needs a **fluid** (liquid or gas) to transfer the heat energy.

Convection moves air and water, creating wind and ocean currents. It is the difference in temperature that creates the movement. Warm air or water rises, while cool air or water sinks. This circular movement creates convection currents. Winds are convection currents in the air. Ocean currents are convection currents in the water.

The movement starts because of uneven heating. We know some areas of Earth are warmer than others. But the movement continues in a **cycle.** The warm air or water transfers its heat to the cooler air or water. So temperatures keep changing, and the movement keeps going.

Make a convection current

Make some ice cubes using water that has food coloring mixed into it to make a strong color. Fill a jar with hot water. Add one of the colored ice cubes, and watch what happens. In this experiment, the water is unevenly cooled rather than unevenly heated. However, it has a similar effect to uneven heating. The movements you see in the water are convection currents.

Patterns in the wind

There are patterns to the world's winds and currents. The systems can change in detail, but overall they stay the same.

Global wind patterns are caused by the way the air is heated by the Sun. The air at the equator gets the most heat. This warm air rises, and cooler air from the north and south moves in to take its place. This produces a pattern of winds blowing toward the equator. The spin of Earth bends the direction of the winds, so they do not blow directly north and south. There are similar patterns in the winds further from the equator.

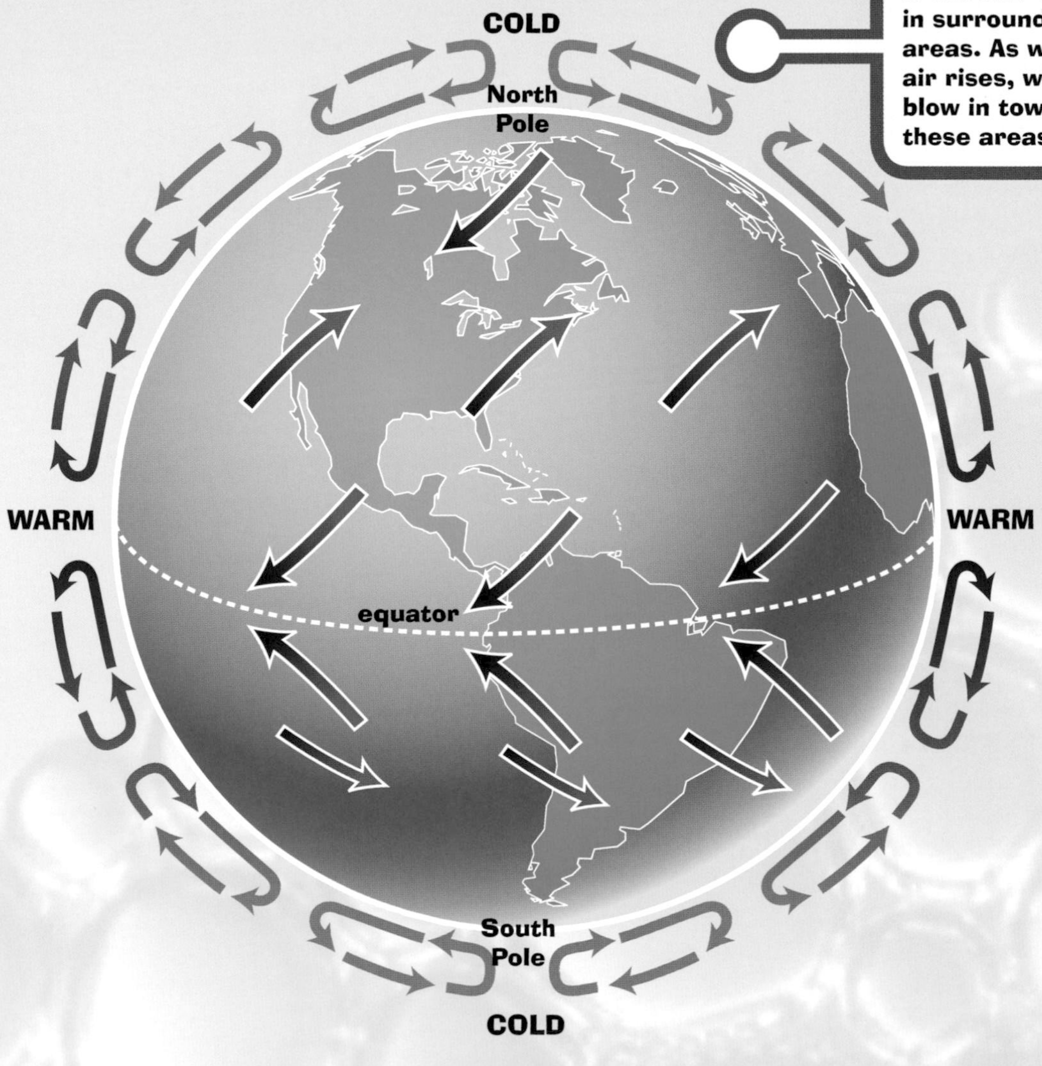

The world's winds follow a regular pattern, shown here. Near the equator, the air is warmer than in surrounding areas. As warm air rises, winds blow in towards these areas.

COLD

North Pole

WARM

WARM

equator

South Pole

COLD

Hurricane energy

Hurricanes have an amazing amount of energy. They can move air at a speed of 160 kilometers per hour (100 miles per hour). One hurricane can pick up 10 billion metric tons (11 billion tons) of water! When the water falls over land in torrents of rain, it can cause terrible floods.

Land and sea breezes

Local winds can be different from larger-scale weather patterns. An example is the daily pattern of land and ocean breezes. It can be fairly windy by the ocean, which is why kitesurfing is so popular! By day, the land warms more quickly than the ocean. Air over the land becomes warmer than air over the ocean. The warm air rises, and cooler air from the ocean blows in to take its place. At night, the pattern is reversed. The land cools more quickly than the ocean. The warmer, rising air is now over the ocean. Cooler air from the land blows out to take its place.

Ocean currents

As we saw with winds, ocean currents are caused by uneven heating. Where the ocean gets warmer, the water expands, and the ocean level rises. Water flows down from these higher areas to lower, cooler areas.

Other processes also affect ocean currents. As the water moves, the spin of Earth makes it turn. The water moves in great circular currents called **gyres**.

Salt levels

The salinity (saltiness) of the ocean affects its movements, just as temperatures do. Because of **climate change**, ice from land is melting into the oceans. This freshwater (water without high levels of salt) will change the level of salt in the oceans. The change in salinity will alter the oceans' currents.

You can clearly see the spiral shape of a gyre off the east coast of Japan in this **satellite** image.

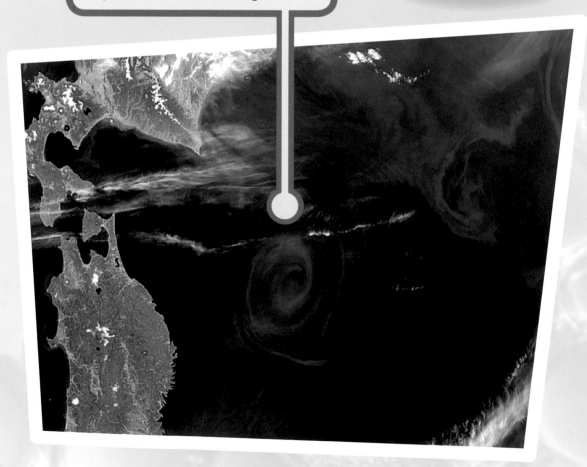

Creating the weather

Winds, water, and uneven heating combine to produce our weather and **climate**. We saw in the water cycle (pages 14 and 15) how the atmosphere can take up water when it gets warm. Winds carry this warm, wet air to other areas. When the air cools, it can no longer hold so much water, and rain falls. If it is cold enough, the rain may become hail or snow.

Air temperature affects the air pressure (the push of air on a surface it touches). Air pressure has important effects on weather. Where air is warming and rising, there is low pressure at ground level. As the air rises, it often **condenses** (changes to liquid). So low-pressure areas often have clouds and rain.

Where air is cooling and sinking, an area of high pressure forms at ground level. High pressure often brings fair weather and less chance of rain.

All the Earth's cycles and systems are connected to others. When snow falls, it is part of the water cycle. It is also part of other systems and cycles, such as the seasons.

Learning from
Satellites

How do we know about the air and water systems? How can we see their effect on Earth? Satellites that orbit the planet give scientists useful information about our climate.

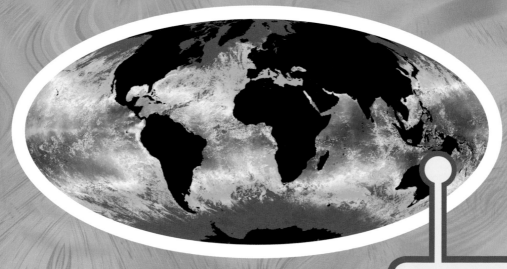

Measuring temperature

Some satellites send images made from **infrared radiation** (heat). They can be even more useful than visual images. Experts can use infrared images to work out land and sea temperatures. They also can trace ocean currents and measure the heights of clouds.

This temperature map of the world's oceans was made from satellite images. The red areas show warmer surface temperatures, yellows and greens are in the middle range, and blues show cold water.

Studying the weather and climate

Weather satellites send information back to Earth from way out in space. By day, photographs and other images sent from satellites can show where clouds and storms are developing. Satellites can show us fires, volcanic eruptions, and pollution.

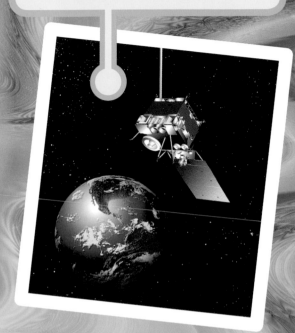

Geostationary weather satellites monitor Earth's surface. They gather data and can provide warnings of severe weather patterns.

With a satellite's view from space, we can learn a lot about our planet. A meteorite (chunk of rock falling from space) several hundred million years ago left scars in the Sahara Desert. The area of impact shows up in this satellite image. It is about 22 kilometers by 28 kilometers (about 14 miles by 17 miles) in size.

SATELLITE ORBITS

Weather satellites circle Earth in two different orbits (paths around a planet). Some are in a polar orbit. They circle Earth constantly in a north-south orbit. They can take pictures of the whole planet. Other satellites are in **geostationary orbit**. These satellites orbit at the same speed as the world turns. They appear to stay over one spot on the ground. A geostationary satellite can "watch" a large area all the time, but there are parts of Earth's surface that it never "sees."

Cycles, Systems, and Us

Earth's cycles and systems are powerful forces. When they are in balance, the processes needed for life can take place. But it appears that human actions are affecting that balance.

How can people have such an impact? It is because there are so many of us. Almost 7 billion people live on this planet. The demand for land, energy, water, and food is causing change in several cycles.

We saw on pages 20–21 how humans are affecting the **carbon** cycle. Let's look at some other ways people change Earth's cycles.

Too little water

Humans are affecting the balance of the water cycle. We use huge amounts of water to irrigate (provide water for) farmland. Factories and power plants use a lot of water, too. In some areas of the world, water from rivers is sent on a different course for hundreds of miles to supply farms and cities. This causes terrible problems for the areas that lose their natural water supply.

In parts of the Aral Sea, ships that once floated on water are rusting on dry land.

Too much nitrogen

Other cycles are also affected by people's actions. Farming adds a lot of extra **nitrogen** to soil, and it runs into rivers and oceans. It can cause some **phytoplankton** to grow too quickly. This affects food and oxygen supplies for fish and other sea creatures. So by upsetting the nitrogen balance on land, we can harm the oxygen cycle and **food webs** in the sea.

The Aral Sea

The Aral Sea in Uzbekistan and Kazakhstan used to be one of the world's biggest lakes. But in 1960, its water supply was diverted to irrigate farms in central Asia. By 2005, the Aral Sea had lost 75 percent of its water, and it was split into two parts. Fish supplies died off, and thousands of people in the fishing industry lost their jobs. Dust blew off the dry seabed, polluting the air and making people sick. Today, some of the flow to the northern Aral Sea has been restored. The fish are coming back, and the air and water quality have improved.

Cycles and Systems Quiz

Here are some questions about **cycles** and **systems**. See if you remember the answers from what you have read. If not, you'll find them if you look back in the book!

1. Where do plants get their energy from?
   a. From oxygen
   b. From sunlight
   c. From water

2. What is the name of the process by which plants get energy from the Sun?
   a. **Respiration**
   b. **Photosynthesis**
   c. Oxidation

3. How much of the world's water is in the oceans?
   a. More than 30 percent
   b. Less than 0.3 percent
   c. More than 96 percent

4. What is the **geosphere**?
   a. All the ice in Earth's oceans and lands
   b. All the rocks and soil in Earth's surface
   c. All living things in the world

5. What is a **carbon sink**?
   a. A **carbon store** that releases carbon dioxide
   b. A substance made entirely of **carbon**
   c. A carbon store that takes up carbon from the **atmosphere**

6. Which living things can break down rocks?
   a. Lichens
   b. Fungi
   c. Decomposers

7. Where do the ocean's salts come from?
   a. From the air
   b. From **phytoplankton**
   c. From rivers

8. How much water can a hurricane pick up?
   a. 1,000 billion metric tons
   b. 10 billion metric tons
   c. 1,000 metric tons

See page 47 for answers.

Glossary

accumulate build up

algae simple, plantlike life forms that live in water and have no roots or seeds

atmosphere layer of gases that surrounds Earth and other planets

atom small piece of matter that everything is made up of

bacteria microscopic, single-celled organisms

biogeochemical (BGC) having to do with the living and nonliving worlds and the chemical reactions that take place among them

biomass all matter that comes from living things, including animal remains and plant materials

biosphere all living things on Earth

carbon element found in all living things as well as in some nonliving substances, such as coal and oil

carbon sink store of carbon that takes up carbon from the atmosphere

carbon source store of carbon that emits carbon into the atmosphere

carbon store any place or thing that contains and holds carbon, such as the ocean, the atmosphere, and plants

chemical reaction process of change that takes place when one substance combines with and responds to another

climate overall weather patterns of a region over a long time

climate change changes caused by the gradual warming of Earth's climate

combustion chemical reaction that makes things burn, caused by combining fuel with oxygen

compound substance made up of more than one kind of atom

condense change from a gas into a liquid

convection movement of fluid due to warmer fluids rising and cooler fluids sinking

current pattern of water flowing through the ocean like a river

cycle network of processes that follow a repeating pattern

element simple substance made of just one kind of atom

emission substance released into the air, such as gases released by the burning of fossil fuels

equator imaginary line that goes around the middle of Earth at an equal distance from the North and South poles

erosion movement of rock and sediments by gravity, water, ice, or wind

evaporate change from a liquid into a gas

fluid gas or liquid

food chain system in which one living thing is a food source for the next in the chain

food web network in which energy flows from the Sun through all living things as they get eaten by other living things and pass on their energy

fossil fuels fuels, including coal, natural gas and petroleum (oil), that contain carbon and were formed underground from plant and animal matter

geosphere all of the rocks and soil that make up Earth's outer layer

geostationary orbit type of circular path taken in which a satellite orbits at the same speed as Earth turns and so appears to stay in one spot

groundwater water that is held in rocks underground

gyre something that forms a spiral or circle or that moves in a spiral motion, especially a circular ocean current

hydrosphere Earth's water system, including ice, oceans, and all water in the atmosphere and on or in the ground

igneous rock rock formed by the hardening of melted rock

infiltration movement of water from the surface of Earth into rocks below the ground

infrared having to do with the rays that we commonly refer to as heat

limestone sedimentary rock made from the shells of ancient ocean animals

magma rock that has melted into a thick liquid

metamorphic rock rock formed by pressure and heat

mineral element or compound that occurs naturally in Earth's surface. Rocks are made up of minerals, and many minerals are extracted from them. Many substances, from oil and salt to metals and gemstones, are minerals.

molecule group of atoms joined together

nitrogen element that in the form of a gas makes up much of the air in Earth's atmosphere

nutrient substance that helps plants and animals to grow

organism any living thing

particle small piece of matter

photosynthesis process by which plants and phytoplankton make food from carbon dioxide, sunlight, and water

phytoplankton microscopic organisms that live in the ocean and use photosynthesis

precipitation moisture falling to Earth in the form of rain or snow

radiation energy given off by atoms as invisible waves or particles

resources useful things, including natural resources such as wood or oil

respiration breathing process during which animals take in oxygen from the atmosphere or from water

runoff flow of water that is not absorbed by soil but that flows into drains, rivers, lakes, or the ocean

satellite object that travels in a circle around another object, and especially human-made objects sent into space to orbit Earth

sediment settled material

sedimentary rock rock formed when sediments collect and are squashed over a long period

system group of parts that connect to each other and work as a whole

tissues groups of similar cells that work together in plants or animals

transpiration process during which plants release water through their leaves

weathering wearing away of rock surfaces or other hard surfaces caused by the weather

Find Out More

Books

Desonie, Dana. *Hydrosphere: Freshwater Systems and Pollution*. New York: Chelsea House Publications, 2008.

Harman, Rebecca. *Carbon-Oxygen and Nitrogen Cycles: Respiration, Photosynthesis, and Decomposition*. Chicago: Heinemann, 2005.

Harman, Rebecca. *The Earth's Weather: Changing Patterns and Systems*. Chicago: Heinemann, 2005.

Wojahn, Rebecca Hogue and Donald Wojahn. *A Desert Food Chain: A Who-Eats-What Adventure in North America*. Minneapolis, MN: Lerner, 2009.

Websites

eo.ucar.edu/kids/green/
Living in the Greenhouse
Explore some more aspects of Earth's climate and cycles.

nasascience.nasa.gov/kids/earth-science-for-kids
Earth from Space
Look at amazing satellite images of Earth and navigate through the water cycle.

www.geography4kids.com/files/atm_intro.html
Geography4kids.com—Atmosphere
Find out why the atmosphere is so important to life on Earth.

www.minsocam.org/MSA/k12/rkcycle/rkcycleindex.html
MSA's Rock'n Internet Site—the Rock Cycle!
Learn more about the different types of rock in the rock cycle.

Topics to research

Use the websites and books listed above to find out more about cycles and systems. You could make a list of all the cycles you learned about in this book. Then you could look at how they affect each other. For example, what effect does the water cycle have on the rock cycle? How does the carbon cycle work with the oxygen cycle or the food web?

Quiz Answers

1. **b** 2. **b** 3. **c** 4. **b** 5. **c** 6. **a** 7. **c** 8. **b**

Index

accumulation 9, 15
air systems 34, 35, 36, 37, 39, 40
animals 4, 12, 13, 32, 33
   and carbon 16, 17
   decay of 23, 33
   and nitrogen 24, 25
   ocean 18, 19, 22, 23, 43
   and oxygen 22, 23
   and water 15
atmosphere 5, 11, 15, 39
   and carbon 16, 17, 18, 20,
      31, 33
   and nitrogen 24, 25
   and oxygen 22, 23
   and Sun's energy 28, 29,
      31, 34

bacteria 22, 24, 25, 33
biogeochemical (BGC) cycles
   10–13, 16
biosphere 5, 22

carbon 6, 11, 16, 33
carbon cycle 16–17, 42
carbon dioxide 6, 7, 16,17, 18,
   20, 31, 33
carbon stores 18, 19
chemical reactions 7, 10, 22
climate change 20–21, 30, 38
condensation 14, 15, 39
convection currents 34, 35,
   36, 38
currents 4, 21, 28, 34, 35, 36,
   38, 40

elements 6, 11, 16, 24, 26
energy 12, 32
   balance of 28–31
   from the Sun 5, 7, 12,
      28–31, 32
erosion 26, 27
evaporation 15

food 7, 12, 17, 24, 25, 32, 33, 42
food chain 32
food web 32–33, 43
fossil fuels 17, 19, 20, 31

geosphere 5, 22
greenhouse gases 20

hurricanes 37
hydrosphere 5, 22

ice 8, 9, 14, 30, 38
infiltration 15

life cycles 11, 12, 13

movement
   of air 34, 35, 36, 37
   on Earth 4, 6, 8, 9, 10, 34
   of rocks 4, 6, 8, 12, 26, 27
   of water 4, 5, 8, 12, 14, 15,
      34, 35, 38, 39

nitrogen 11, 24, 43
nitrogen cycle 24–25, 43

oceans and seas 4, 9, 11, 14,
   15, 22, 27, 37, 40, 43
   and carbon 16, 17, 18, 19
   and oxygen 23
   and Sun's energy 28, 29,
      34, 38
   See also currents.
oxygen 6, 7, 11, 43
oxygen cycle 22, 43

photosynthesis 7, 12, 22, 23,
   30, 33
phytoplankton 18, 23, 30, 43
plants 4, 7, 9, 12, 30, 32, 33
   and carbon 16, 17, 19

decay of 17, 23, 33
   and nitrogen 24
   and oxygen 22, 23
   and water 15
precipitation 15

radiation 28, 29, 30, 31, 40
respiration 12, 15, 17, 33
rock cycle 11, 26–27
rocks 4, 8, 9, 29
   and carbon 16, 17, 18, 19
   and oxygen 22, 23
   types of 27
runoff 15

satellites 18, 38, 40–41
seasons 4, 5, 11, 34, 39
sediments 17, 18, 27
soil 5, 16, 24, 25, 33
Sun, the 5, 11, 28, 29, 30,
   31, 32

tides 4
transpiration 15

uneven heating 28, 29, 30,
   31, 34, 35, 36, 39

volcanoes 16, 27, 41

water 29, 42, 43
   amount of 8, 14
   salt 8, 9, 38
   states of 8, 14, 15, 39
   storage of 9, 14, 15
   systems 34, 35, 38, 40
water cycle 5, 11, 14–15, 39
weather 4, 34, 39, 41
weathering 26, 27
wind 4, 9, 28, 34, 35, 36, 37, 39